by

illustrated by Roz Fulcher

Harcourt
SCHOOL PUBLISHERS

Printed in China

ISBN 10: 0-15-358466-1
ISBN 13: 978-0-15-358466-4
Ordering Options
ISBN 10: 0-15-358357-6 (Grade K Above-Level Collection)
ISBN 13: 978-0-15-358357-5 (Grade K Above-Level Collection)
ISBN 10: 0-15-360696-7 (package of 5)
ISBN 13: 978-0-15-360696-0 (package of 5)

4 5 6 7 8 9 10 0940 15 14 13 12 11 10 09

Zim and Zan buzz.

They want a job.

Where can they get a job?

Sam can fix a web.

Can Zim and Zan do that job?

They can not do it. They can

not fix a web.

Sam can get a bug.

Can Zim and Zan do that job?

They can not do it. They can
not get a bug.

4

Al can dig and dig.

Can Zim and Zan do that job?

They can not do it. They can not dig.

Al can zip in and out.

Can Zim and Zan do that job?

They can not do it. They can not zip.

"Look up there."

"Is this a good job for us?"

"Can we do it?"

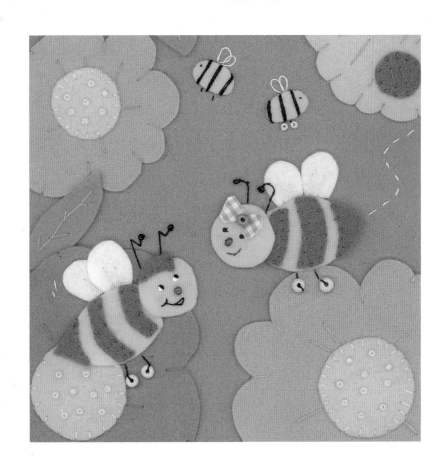

"Yes, we can!"

This is the job for a bee.

It is a good job for Zim and Zan.